D1739040

THE GLOWING RIVER

THE GLOWING RIVER

new & selected poems by

JACK MYERS

— • —

CONTEMPORARY CLASSICS POETRY SERIES
INVISIBLE CITIES PRESS • MONTPELIER, VERMONT

Invisible Cities Press
50 State Street
Montpelier, VT 05602
www.invisiblecitiespress.com

Library of Congress Cataloging-in-Publication Data

Myers, Jack Elliott, 1941–
The glowing river : new & selected poems / by Jack Myers
cm. – (Contemporary classics poetry series)
ISBN 0-9679683-9-9 (cloth : alk. paper)
ISBN 1-931229-10-4 (paper : alk. paper)
I. Title. II. Series.

PS3563.Y42 G58 2001
81'.54—dc21   2001016610

Manufactured in the United States of America

Book design by
Peter Holm
Sterling Hill Productions

FIRST EDITION

CONTENTS

THE GLOWING RIVER

The Glowing River

The spin I'd put on my father's wanting to be alone
would be to compare him to solitary males of the wild kingdom
whose nobility and courage disdained the flock, the herd,
the whole squawking barbecue of fear and indecision.

But when I look his isolation in the eye I see
he couldn't love easily, though he felt so deeply
he spent all his life resisting it,

like the nuclear power plant that recycled so much warm water
it choked on weeds, so they stocked the lake with weed-eating fish
who, in my mind, prospered so well that I knew soon something
larger, more ominous and foreign would arrive.

They would gather at the mouth of the underwater river
and, basking in the heat of its eerie, greenish glow,
fall asleep under the spell of an alien sun.

You see the problem, how the unnatural, over time, spawns something
stranger than we'd meant. Which is why I'm studying my nature through
what must've happened to my father. Toxic secrets beyond the mouth
of the glowing river I'll never learn but like all sons have put my faith in.

—•—•—•—

New Poems

(1999 – Present)

Parable of the Burden

When I was little I loved to be good,
loved to be of use to whoever could use me.

I held the world's record
for the fastest errands in my family
and only the most suicidal grains of mica
would flash when I swept.

"He's good, he's so good," my parents whispered
like pickpockets, as if I were a tourist who
dropped his wallet.
Each day was a cargo of goods I expected
to send sailing out of sight.

That's when I decided to be "difficult,"
though everyone I loved back then
died waiting for me to grow up.

Who wouldn't be good, I thought,
if pleasing others could ease the burden
of being good, if like those great transcendent souls,
or me when I was little, I could've lifted those burdens
like a toast to and from and for myself.

— • • • —

Whatever You Do

It is said the difference between
the adept and the child
lighting a candle is that
one acts as if he has never seen
the power fire has to return anything
it touches to light
while the other seems transfixed
as if something beautiful
were being illuminated inside him.

But it did not say which was which.

———•••———

Life Boat

There's been a lot of fighting
in this little boat
though I've been as alone
as before I was born.

I've split the gunnels,
widened the cracks,
and the stern is pulling away.

That's why I'm afraid
of putting out to sea
with or without it,

still bickering about how
my little journey
still stuck in sand
should and shouldn't be.

—•—•—•—

Mindfulness

The vase that confuses the feeling
of water filling it up
with the water filling it up
is no longer a vase.

But the vase that remains a vase
while feeling like water filling it up
is also a flower.

—•—•—•—

Pets

My three dogs follow me wherever I go.
I should name them for my hungers:
Worry Wart, Run Away, Never Wake Up.

I should tell them *There's no place like home,*
that *Life is beautiful and precious,*
and *What will be will be.*

But that's what I was told by my parents
when I hungered, as if they were ancient Chinese
who fished by tying nooses around the throats
of cormorants they kept.

Now I pay tribute to my hungers.
I unplug the hole in the fence to honor breaking out;
I let sleeping dogs lie to protest the indignities of living;
I go outside the house and bang on the walls,
and demand to be let in.

Now, the cliches that contained them
are the freedoms I contain. But better yet,
my dogs are just my dogs again.

—•—•—•—

The Tao of Light

When I learned that "Black Radiation"
is the invisible emission of light
by a hot solid, such as the human body,
which is also a perfect absorber of light,

I realized I've lived in the shadow
of whatever I didn't see,
and that the light I cast made shadows out of
wherever I happened to be.

So when The Bible says God separated light
from darkness—meaning darkness is not just
the absence of light—the answer to the question
"What is the opposite of light?"
turns out to depend on who's doing the talking
and who they're talking to.

—•—•—•—

The Flicker

This is in honor of the flicker
that sings its heart out on my roof everyday
though no other flicker comes.

If I can't be sure of the language of joy
can I at least know what is?

There is a flicker flapping its wings and playing
with the name of whatever it's doing.

The tiny bit of him that weighs something
is holding down the house

while the larger part of him that weighs nothing
lifts it up.

—•—•—•—

Spring

A male cardinal has been flaunting his repertoire
in the hackberry outside my window. It goes like this:

First his aria, a series of squeaky clean, individually
cellophane-wrapped water droplets bursting like
hothouse tomatoes into the King's English.

Then his knee-slapping raunchy Appalachian kazoo-tooting series
which, if I were interested, would sound stable as a beetle.

Then silence—as if he's listening for the phone to ring—
answered by a longer, much more patient feminine silence.

Maybe I'm projecting here as he re-begins more quietly,
but has self-doubt set in? Sounds like he's ordered a table-
for-one, but hasn't yet touched his pink champagne and grits.

God, this is heartbreaking.
Maybe he's not good-looking.
How well I remember that being
a major aspect of natural selection.

No, the quieter song's not about his sadness,
it's from another bird who seems wiser.
Maybe he's married.

I can't see anything. For all I know what I've heard
is my rusty air conditioner. My wife, who I chased after
and managed to land after exhausting intercontinental courtings,
says my special gift is to say what no one else imagines
while doing my daily 360s on my branch.

—•—•—•—

Building the Temple

I would like to build a temple
out of stone
by the sea.

A place to meditate and practice
harnessing the power
of surrender.

But I can't carve or sculpt.

If I looked as long as it would take
to learn to sculpt,
I could find the rocks that fit,

rocks whose religious faces pouring over them
surpassed art, and whose imaginings of peace
were just as difficult as carving.

But having faith the rocks are there
and fit whatever I imagine, is,
in a way, building the temple.

—•—•—•—

untitled

When I find myself wanting
to be famous for what little talent I possess,
I compose the best poem I can
on two halves of a potato
in my head.

—•—•—•—

Now

Wouldn't it be horrible to live life backwards,
be born old with all your wisdom and faith,
knowledge and achievements,
gradually sinking like the Himalayas back into liquid?

Each day in the bazaar, the heart, lost in the swirl
of its entourage and finery, passes by the soul
hidden inside her black *chador*.

Traipsing back and forth, the heart thinks
he can create *déjà vu* by force.
And the soul, poor thing, being everywhere at once,
doesn't know backwards from forwards.

—•—•—•—

I Don't Want You to Feel Listened to

Lately, I've been listening to the sound of your laughter
rising like a laddering of birds in the sky.

But I'm not going to tell you this.
Birds who feel loved and safe
eventually can't fly.

But you know me, the only kind of fact I believe in
is like me in my underwear being whipped around
like the last bird in your skywriting laughter.

You're on fire all the time!
You're an open window!
How come you chose me?

—•—•—•—

The Sequin

What are you waiting for in the future,
for when you'll be able to beam yourself anywhere at will?

You'll still be like a child awe-struck in your parents' wardrobe,
feeling powerless because their sparkling garments of desire

come through louder and clearer than they do. It's about being anything
other than who you are, isn't it?

You are a sunbeam shot from the sun
at a sequin on your mother's dress
whose purpose is to cover her body
by catching the light. To glamorize
and dazzle the eye and stir desire for another.

Toward what purpose?

—•—•—•—

Incarnation

A friend of mine won't eat pork because pigs are so intelligent.
Another won't eat anything higher than an egg.
And still another won't eat anything with a face.

But I've seen gnats fall in love with other gnats across a crowded room.
I've seen a single seed lift tons of wood above its head.
And don't some of my best ideas come from meditating on rocks?

So, please, whoever has the true and secret knowledge, tell us what to eat.

Remind us, when we lift our knife and fork in praise of our transcendence
    over everything
beneath us, that there are forces that can crystallize mist
into exquisite works of ice that love melting back to mist again.

Remind us, before we eat, that we are monumental,
momentary works of mist. And that everything and everyone
who has ever existed has brought us here.

—•—•—•—

On Purpose

How victoriously the iron nail resists
the dividing wills of wind and wood.

As perfectly as its slow corruption will complete
its resistance to what it is.

—•—•—•—

The Blackening

—for Jessie

My daughter's best friend gave her
purple silk pajamas as a birthday gift.

Whirling around in them, she blends
the heart of their Persian designer
through the spools of their Chinese seamstress
to the K-Mart lady circling her nubile manikin.

She's looking for her Friend
in the heart of the young man
the dreams of these pajamas
have begun to manifest.

I celebrate this. But I also feel its shadow rise
into the eclipse the priests of the old religions invoked
in prohibiting such gifts
when they obliterated the young man they once were
who was still whirling, as young as ever, inside them.

—•—•—•—

Alchemy

My neighbor's trying to start his truck.
It coughs and sputters and backfires several times
before it finally starts up. The sound of it

says he's financially strapped yet considerate
in the way he soothes and brushes the gas
to a quiet idle so early in the morning

as if he knew the sweet messages from his wild
and penniless past are bolted to harbingers
of what will come next.

He thinks if he can get it to turn over
he'll get one more day to start. But he doesn't understand
my work, which is to sit and see what's next.

How can I explain my work is to become my neighbor,
and then while still in my pajamas looking like me sitting here, become
his truck?

—•—•—•—

The Never-Mind Life

After dropping a tranquilizer on the rug,
which coated it with hair and dust,

I blew it off and, instead of taking it,
I put it back in the jar and shook it twice.

This way I made sure I'd never know
when I'd choose the dirty one again.

Or, now maybe all of them would be tainted
the way things taste after brushing your teeth.

Or, possibly, having jostled it around with the others,
the pill would somehow clean itself.

It wasn't what you'd call a "life-threatening situation,"
but from now on the whole pill-taking thing would get complex.

—•—•—•—

She Didn't Know and He Never Said

She didn't know he planted marigolds outside
their window anymore than he could see the flowers
she dreamed of while she slept, or that when she took
a shower, which is how she spoke, by saying everything
at once, he made it a point never to flush the toilet;
how he silently withstood the daily firing squad
of his most bored students who, like the Xmas gifts she bought
year round, that gleamed hidden in her closet,
he kept unconscious.

He was reared to show his love like the mythical octopus
who, neglected and starved, ate itself up—
first an arm, then another and another, then its head—
until it lived as an undying presence turned inside out
in a corner of its murky aquarium, living off the sadness
inside the little things he never said and she didn't notice
which held them together and came to assume a life
of their own, making life seem mysterious, a little better.

— • — • — • —

Smoke Break

The students walk by me, their destinies
morphed into faces like homework
on how the journey's been so far.

I seem to be invisible to them.
So most of me must look like
what I am in the world.

It's the best way to see the ambition and lust
and wreckage of mistakes splashed down like blossoms
from a dirt storm into a road.

When I was young and one of them, everyone's face
seemed alien. Now I want to shout out help
and encouragement, give piggybacks to happiness away.

But I could use a little help myself to get the last proud bit of me
invisible: Selenia Rosario Colon, when I drove by your orphanage
that huge thing at the end of glory that felt like humility

passed through me like the wind of these struggling faces, leaving behind
the irreducible and stubbornest part of me I can't surrender to,
the part that asked if we could stop.

—•—•—•—

Eyelash on a Piece of Jade

After 5,000 years
one would think
that Asian artists
would lose interest in
the white lotus
floating on a pond
beneath a distant mountain peak

as if they were saying only stillness
can capture the quickest, the slightest
blink of that maiden
lying in a bamboo thicket
blown down and spreading out
from the long black sigh of her hair,

that the paradox "What stays is what doesn't last"
is the paradox of art.

I inhale the smoke trail of my cigarette
fanning out into the wide blue sky
back into a cigarette again,
melt back before my birth
to the lust my father felt
for my mother in Hokku province, 1941,

after he surprised her
with a piece of rare green jade
she left to my wife
who took it off last night
after we argued and stayed home
on our weekly special night out
we promised to reserve just for us.

———• • •———

The Great Work

> *Then Dr. Bluespire . . . whispered into [the ape's] ear:*
> *"You look like a god sitting there.*
> *Why don't you try writing something?"*
>
> —James Tate, "Teaching the Ape to Write Poems"

I've spent my whole life searching for magic: overcame
my pounding heart in order to lift my astral foot above my head
and correctly guess the queen of hearts which my ex-wife said
she always held above her head; focused all my force of mind
to rattle a teacup in its saucer when I could've done it with my foot.

But I cherish those meditations, even when I fell asleep,
those long involved fallings inward and levitations upward
to see what Sis' was up to though I could've used the phone.

But I found if you stare a fact in the face down to its fractals,
the real can be intuited; and even though you pass right by
the obvious and maybe get embarrassed, it still feels magical.

Have I come full circle just to say in the mist of a "senior moment," *Now
what was it I was looking for?* Am I the prodigal fish who
spent his life searching for the magical thing called water?

But when your knees lock up looking for some change you dropped
and you find your long lost glasses, it makes the ordinary miraculous.

Maybe I could've hopped another life and arrived where I already am,
but there's something I can't quite remember, like a Post-it note
stuck on a fridge in another life that says "You're special," though it

might've said "Get pickles." Even mistakes are magical.
Like all the adepts have said for ages, it's the getting what I've got
and the getting where I am that makes real life feel magical.

—•—•—•—

The Deep Blue Sea of Surrender

When the fisherman who wouldn't let go
hooked the fish who wouldn't get caught,
who he thought he was and what he wasn't
was the line whose job it was to snap
so they wouldn't tear themselves apart.

So they wouldn't tear themselves apart
each lived inside the illusion of who
was fishing and who was caught,
and, when the line snapped, what was lost.

—•—•—•—

The Iridescent Flashings of the Integral One

—after Thich Nhat Hahn

The acid pages of my book on consciousness
are eating their way back home toward the fields of rain and sun, and
hands and languages
they came from.

A moment ago, thin as this paper's edge,
the page gave way to Lao Tsu 2,000 years ago

who predicted I would come, and explained by that how things never
stop being what they are
in the process of becoming what they were.

—•—•—•—

Catching the Hummingbird

It's so lush here now,
as flush as I was last night on wine
summoning up my wild Bird of Paradise.

Everything I planted last year
was bushes and vines and grasses,
whatever would thrive on my distraction
and survive being uprooted and moved
and re-moved until what was left looked like
an orchestra arranged by a tornado.

I'd like to plant something quiet now
above the commotion of wild grasses
to attract the mythic hummingbird,
some tufts of green not-doing, the wine-blue
flowering of what blossoms beyond waiting,
the orange-golden-throated trumpet flowers
of sitting still so I can sneak up on it,
catch a glimpse of it, then prune the glimpsing
from the glimpse.

—•—•—•—

Star Trek

There are three hundred trillion stars
for every man, woman, and child on Earth.
God made just enough for us to wish on.
But not enough to stop my worrying about death.

My last project was practicing being immortal,
picturing eons of blue light-years
through which I let light take over being
the emergency. But it only slowed down whatever I shot past.

Then I stopped at a traffic light
where a blind woman gave me the look
that said we'll all be light soon enough.

Now I'm working on the opposite of what a black hole is,
being in the here-and-now so much I'm everywhere at once.
But it requires cleansing the Golden Flower of Clouded Consciousness,
training the breath to break the mind's obsessive speech.
But the hardest part will be trying to stop smoking first.

—•—•—•—

Hanging Water

—for David Akiba

A photograph of winter branches
        hanging over a lake
            reflecting branches reaching into sky.

    Self-portrait,
        speech of shadow-ink on water,
           speech of light to dark.

Where the branches dipped their tips into their reflection,
    infusing what they are into what they will become,
        there was a momentary, single ripple on the lake
           that stood for everything.

—•—•—•—

from

The Family War

(1977)

Night inside the Hunter

The pale grass waved me away: *Not here.*
The clouds turned over on their backs
like fat bored men and floated off.
But I laid my will along my eyesight
and squeezed off steps until a covey
of birds exploded like buckshot, arching
into the next field where they landed
cocked again, ready to go off.

I know the power of standing still.
How patience flies past flight.
While the red oaks burned downrange
like torches, I spun a hole the size of
the sky in a black twit's brain.
Dog holds my wishes gently in his mouth.

Then we saw a house that looked like God's.
The windows were smashed, a truck upturned,
and a bed lodged halfway down the stairs.
I lifted up and rolled over a rabbit
the size of my heart with my first shot
then entered the house.

As my shadow rose against the wall
I felt my heart stand still.
Something small and hard and bright
travelling all my life opened up in me
a hole the size of myself.
I reloaded and the house fell down like night.

—•—•—•—

Farmer

He counted himself no different
from the rain driving on
the houses, melting down
the stiff lives rocking
in their attics.
When his anger nailed up
the house too small and tight
he would grab for the hard
candies and close his hand
around his son's.

He remembered the helplessness
of a black hawk beating upwards
being jabbed by a faster bird;
how his second-hand bed
still held the broad shape
of another man. He tried hard
because the dirt did.
He knew his rest was coming
from a long way off
and what great thing shone
inside it, he figured, was him.

—• • •—

Wing to Root

When the sun tilts back wing to root
in a fierce sleep, the birds inhabit
the branches like doubts. They soak
in the dusk rocking themselves into
small blind possessions of the wood
and sing one note into the falling
temperature. By dawn they are black
fruit hanging from the bark you think
looks so much like anger. It is home.

—•—•—•—

The Family War

My father made meals underwater
while the war went on. He stirred
enormous pots of S.O.S. in the belly
of a ship, and thinking of me held upside
down, he flipped an extra dash of salt
into the stew as the big guns pushed
and recoiled like a woman in labor.

There was a war, the smell of irons
steaming in small apartments and sons
aiming wooden rifles at each other.
There was Ma grown big-bellied with me
facing the windy sea. That double image
of waiting, Dad, a cold shuttling ocean
throwing up stones and salt.

Then you came back and blocked up all
the windows in the house until my brother
threw the first punch through a wall.
You felt at home, then, coming at us
in the darkness like a slug
from the big guns ready to explode.

——•—•—•——

An Old Story for My 3-Year-Old Son

—for Ben

To calm you down we let you tear off
great chunks of sleep. The iron settles
in your waterglass, the small bubbles bear
weightlessness to the light and a quiet
sign is posted in the street. We try hard
to keep your beautiful small face oblivious
to the roomful of Viennese observers chanting
Penis, Cosmos, Power, Cancer, Kiss, until
that white noise, that scream of yours, breaks
the driest voice among to its knees.

We understand so much. The closed door,
the windy punishments and rewards pour from
wrinkled grab-bags, these hands I've trained
your eyes on. Near the end of my defeat
I'll tell you how they sent a few sad hoofbeats
on the roof that changed positions like my debts,
all back and legs with no head. How I climbed
on top of this blue shivering nag, splitting
my sides from the annual bad joke, my job,
grubbing through ashes and bricks, lonely,
freezing, driven crazy by helpers. How even
the grass flew in its place to keep your green.
My folks gave me a recording of their screams.
It is so perfect, it is why I guard your sleep.

———•—•—•———

When I Held You to My Chest, You Fit

At first I was worried about you
liking me. Doesn't every father
think of zoos and long rides
into the interior of his child?

So I took you to the elephant
that held a telephone pole
above his head and swam toward us
with his human eye that said
"This is what I do, and you?"

You didn't see him; instead you studied
the specks of rust around his cage
and ate a few. Then you wept
for the small snail stuck under his foot.
I, too, have crawled the underside

of bars watching the sad faces
of gum harden into one color.
I know how we belong together:
When I see the Big View, you see
how it hides its thousand hearts.

—•••—

Wind and Soup

For six days I've been reheating soup.
The bird in the soup never flew,
never complained unless you would call
the red flesh of his head a complaint.

I ask my son where we come from.
He says the wind.
When he couldn't fly he told me
little people helped him
pour darkness into holes.
And where are we going?
The wind.

The grease breaks up and melts in the heat.
The house sleeps
and I begin to care for the soup.

What will I do when it's gone?
I thought nothing of the parts of my body
until they were injured.
Each remembers its history of aches,
the holes in my teeth, the cracked wrist
and head, parts lopped off,
the clean new openings. The parts remember
when they did something perfectly
though it was useless.
All this will fit into the wind.

Soon there'll be nothing left to do
but make something else old.
Love it no matter what
I may do with it,
ask if it's the same each day
as each piece falls apart and is absorbed
by another, then by me
until there is no distinction left
between me and it. Wind and soup.

—•—•—•—

Sunbathing

We've reached the ocean and one son
is laughing as he watches the surface
of the water fly back to itself. He's overcoming
fear. The other son is so small and happy,
when he reaches out to strangers, they leave
themselves for love.

My wife and I are on the hard-packed mud
hoping no one knows us. It's hard to explain
our lives, why the invisible make us feel
secure, armored like the crab with feelers
and a trapdoor over its heart.

When no one comes, we know we've come back
to watch our children judge us. They think
we are so perfect, we've brought our bodies out
to burn in the sun.

—• • •—

Nanny's Last Years

—in memory of Belle Cohen

*There are two things you cannot face
steadily, the sun and death.*

—Anonymous

Over the years they've perfected their move
away from me, so I end up kissing the air,
dumpy and hungry, on the lookout to hug
something small to death. I get up early,
watch the sun pull itself over the house,
open my mouth and find that I have slept
again. I find I'm picking at the bones
of a thin whitefish, wintering in Miami,
or visiting my sons on Sunday. They left me
out of their cars, pass me like a soft food
to my grandchildren's lips. Their eyes close
like good children. God knows what they pretend
I am. With the world in their hands they think
they will arrive with the world in their hands.
I tell them pick out what you like and take it
home. I'm tired of wearing out their patience
with my talk of death, shrinking down to this
baby face they lean into and say go back to sleep.

—•—•—•—

Leaving

Each year we pack our things
swearing it's the last time
our kids will see their friends
as broken toys. I take my son
to show him how the bathers are
warming up to cross the world,
how they pour the cold blue sea
in their ears, then swim out
laughing with beautiful bodies.
So he runs flat out with me,
his thin white body like a kite
trying to break its tiny sticks
to win that final letting go.
We pass people like poles along
a track and shout we are leaving,
leaving, we are going all the way.

———• • •———

Blue Collar

I work with men whose laughter
lifted the bar stools through a window
last night. They are burning out
the weaker lives inside them,
hitting the bars as the walls harden
and their hands lose the feel of machines.
They know tomorrow they'll be broke,
that their drinks could've bought the homes
their hands have lifted up and left
for sale. But they unroll their money
and snap it off like farmers
breaking a chicken's neck. Today is home.

——•——•——•——

The Apprentice Painter

I stand there slapping a house
in the face as the young girls
slide by on cool bicycles saying
"Oh, it's only the painters."
No one lets us in. We have to pee
behind trees and eat our one-foot
grinders on the ground.

My Italian boss yells up to me
"Let go of the house! It won't
fall!" I wish the wings of birds
would turn into $20 brushes,
for the hot sun to drop
into the mouth of this house
that screams for more yellow.

Under the table I get good money
to buy more tables with.
I try to think of a better job
but the boss can feel me
dreaming on the other side
of the house and yells
"Don't die on me!"

Each night I lay the new color
of my body down too early,
feeling the dog paws my hands
have become. I dream I'm glad
I'm strong as the boss rides me
from the last job on Earth
to the moon's jumbled houses.

— • • •

Home from the Fish Factory

I keep the punch
in my stomach
intact and come home
feeling like a bus
that's loaded and unloaded
the same dead passenger
at every stop.

My arms hang down
like the long birds
in Chinese shops
and the pinpoints
of light are dying
in both my eyes.

Soon I will sleep
the sleep of the hook
and swing my last
cold flight
over the mouths of the bosses.

———•—•—•———

Numero Uno

When I watch football on TV
the number on an athlete's head
comes true:
the blood behind 32,
the intelligence of 19,
the lanky humor of 12.

But when I'm at the dentist
I can't imagine a number
for myself except last.
The nurse whose dark face
I drill into for understanding
is dressed up like a tooth.
I wear the clothes of a victim
who hopes all his imperfections
don't come loose at once. I tell my wife
that I throw my clothes on the floor
to feel encouraged when they fall.

That's a long way from 56,
brute force, but I haven't fallen
out of bed in weeks.
I stay here daring to fail,
being taunted by calling myself
Number 1 and sweating it out.

—• • •—

The Ant Makes Progress towards Himself

—for Mike Ryan

If the page isn't a hole for escape, you learn
to fill the entrance up with stones and fear
the thunder that comes rolling to roots
of your progress. Sometimes, isn't it always
night, you'll carve your rest into the wall
and yell is this enough? The same thin yell
that told where to dig comes back. Nothing
matters until another tunnel breaks through yours.
Then the shock is seeing someone with your face;
that there's so little left of it, it's grown so dark
it is the blackness shining at the end.

Rerun

Lying with neck against the rattan couch
until my head is numb,
I slide like a loaf of bread
into the warm oven of a late movie
so that I can rise secretly
and return to myself like an excellent decision.

When the actors do badly I melt
into the grey light and change places with them.
I don't see my family for years.

Each channel I enter opens onto myself:
the farmer whose heart is clogged
with the earth he's turned,
the prodigal son returning home
to a house that's been gutted and burned.

The lines fall away as I plow toward
the dark square of night.

What I want to be is what I am.

—•—•—•—

from
I'm Amazed That You're Still Singing
(1981)

Day of Rest

When mother lit the candles on a Friday night
the bull plunging through the rooms all week lay down.
Even the gulls settled down like papers on the breakers.
The Sabbath was the torch she swept her house with.

In those days it was simple: a sip of wine rushed us
through ourselves and we were blessed. The stars
came out like little sayings: Be good. Be good.
It was nothing to touch a God.

But it isn't like that now. The afternoons rise up
like the cement sides of an empty sea and, filling up
on booze, I become the bull. Knock the daylight down.
The walls redden with laughter as I wake up with someone
holding down my fists.

Some Friday night, my last, will find me glazed and stiff.
The light pinched out, last thoughts smoking up
as if I were a wick. Somewhere there'll be a woman
lighting candles and children drinking wine. God bless.
All night there will be a melting into space,
a long, slow leap toward God.

———• • •———

Day of Atonement

On the Day of Atonement we fasted
and threw our money into the sea;
a few faces bright with guilt
went up against the wind
and fell like sinful children
without a splash.

Eventually we lugged God down there
and dumped him in.
It changed the taste of the sea.

Those cold October afternoons seemed carved
out of the light and wind howling
through a ram's horn. Each dry blast
was a mountain in Israel. A word.

When the emptiness in us folded
its corners into a heavy silver star,
we doubled over and feasted on resentment.
Everything taught us how to win.

Once we whispered to each cent
a sin. Now money whispers back.
The emptiness that drilled us out
has hungered, blackened, knotted into sex
until we think of hauling our belongings
down to the sea and following them in.

The waves scrub the sea from Israel
to our feet, as we sway above our lives,
ablaze, wondering how to throw the light in.

———•—•—•———

What's Left

Today I'm going into town to give away what's left.
I drag my memory down like a black wool suit,
let the dead air disrobe from the last sad occasion,
yawn, and inhale the house. It held me as my woman
held me, while the shadows fell and filled my shape.

In the market they will ask did I ever face my life.
Yes, I say. I sat inside it. Only backwards. I watched
the beginning being crushed by landscapes rushing toward it.
Now I toss that in for free, a black dot impossible to lift.

I see the few small things I've gathered in the wagon
make a quiet music. Moored on the warm river in the wood
they nod in the mild wind like grown men settling down,
then they change back into things I can't tell from myself.

At my age I should have one last child and face him
like a mountain. Blind and deaf. Tell him it's easy
to learn when there's nothing left. All this I hitch up
to a strong dumb horse. He will pull it into town,
bearing high his faceful of flies like a torch.

—•—•—•—

The Butcher's Hand

After she executed the laundry
high over an alley, left steam
clinging to the wall,
and transmogrified the hamburg,
my mother called the butcher,
"Cheat, you goddamn thief,"
while I faded through my haze
of prickles as the go-between.

Imagine telling a blood-smeared man
"You're eating out my heart!"
A pound of fresh ground beef
rolled in agony around my basket
as I rode the blood-soaked bag
back. "My mother says this time
you better take your hand off
the scale." I slid along the saw-
dust covered floor, past tongues,
livers, and headless chickens.

Years later I saw my mother's rage
was the rage of the weak, the defeated,
that the butcher heard only drab birds
squawking in the kingdom of disbelief.
Her smashing in the kitchen,
the water rushing through the house,
and the long sigh of exhaustion
when I opened the door was my family
falling like a pound of meat
into the butcher's hand.

The Immigrant

Before I knew your word for *Fall,*
the trees let go beyond the window.
I thought I was rising as the season explained
itself, leaving the streets littered with words.

Then on an August afternoon miles out
on a motionless sea, I lowered down a dropline.
A large cod tugged my hand into the water,
forcing me to see the ripples thin out of sight
until I was staring across the ocean to the east,
feeling it sift through what light was left around me.

That was *evening.* It was like looking into
a woman's eyes and being pulled inside her.
And I could break the spell by swallowing
just as the cod had broken the water
far from my boat. It is impossible to describe
the bareness and dark I drifted through that *night,*
totally outside myself, except to say everything
calms down and becomes whole whenever it offers itself.

There are many other words in the last half of my life
I will learn.

—• • •—

Before Making Love to Me,

she dances the Tai Chi naked,
turning our room 3,000 years old.

The long wind coming toward us
has arrived and I have the feeling

cats are in the room, though nothing
but the moon's white hexagram

has entered through the blinds.
She is sideways in Egyptian relief,

perhaps letting go of birds.
Her breasts dip upward as if just

touched. Her mind is all at once
stills of pouring water, a halted rain

of arrows in a lion, the roar of silence
steaming from an offered dish. I am no more

myself than my clothes hanging in the dark
blue air. She is against me now, as we

move toward making love. The silence,
over the slow explosion of ourselves

rises and falls like blows.

—•—•—•—

To a Distant Lover

It is said
the Zen Archer
never takes a shot
but allows the center
of his target
to expand
until it is night
and small holes
like stars
his arrows
might go through
burst into suns
stuck with arrows.

In the white light
of this night
the Zen Master
becomes
a bow,
an arrow,
the very center
of the target
he flies through.

Accomplishing everything
within nothing,
he complains,
is an exercise
he still must do.

A hundred miles away,
day and night
with one eye closed,
I concentrate on you.

—•—•—•—

Answers

—for Mioko Ito

Today the roses in the silver vase have opened their widest:
red and white faces blown back in a still room.

Even cut, they have the strength to surrender.
Their petals lie scattered like the silks of a courtesan.

I sit here tearing one after another, my thoughts
caught off-guard by my hands.

—•—•—•—

The Instinct

A man feels humiliated
when his wife turns her private
landscape over and leaves him

falling through black space.
There is a horse kicking
in the mind that must be let out.
Men see it in each other's eyes
and hold onto their women.

Young girls who have ridden
this horse in their dreams
cross their legs, still burning,
and concentrate on small talk.

Once in a while, a stray woman
who can get over anything
opens her blouse and teases
the horse into following her home.
As she unlocks the door it occurs to her
how huge it will seem in the house.

Sometimes a man will punish his wife
with abstinence. The horse shrinks
into a small dog who rolls over
the edge of sleep while his master
wanders the house eating leftovers
and shouting to himself.

A woman who hears this
decorates her house and makes breakfast
like a wife in the old days.
She averts her eyes and serves him
a future that is possible
now that he has let her out.

—•—•—•—

The Lover Meets His Desire

He scrubbed the carpet until each nub stood out
like the nipples of a virgin. He polished
the French glasses until they squealed
with the pleasure of holding back.
The ferns rose nobly in a chorus of *ahhs*
and soon the room, elevated in a ringing sound,
was ready.

He squinted into the silence of his expectations
when his ears perked up. He thought the telephone
was about to become hysterical. Suddenly
the room seemed too demanding. Too correct.
So he began living in it as fast as he could.

By the time she arrived, prettied by lateness,
the silence rising from his bed roared
like an iron lung. He stood behind the door
shouting, "Shut up! Shut up!" She questioned
his name ever so softly. Oh how he hated her.

—•—•—•—

Lightweight

The few times I've been knocked out cold
I wasn't interested in coming back. Not that
being a cold black speck in a miasma of stars
was so spectacular, I just couldn't take the fullness
of the heart.

For the heart is a stubborn problem
whose silence is described by noise.
It's the roar of an empty stadium
with the face of a boxer's glove,
the two-fisted pout of a child
who pounds I will and I will not.

So I throw a cold shot down like a fist
smashed in my face. The booze hits my brain
like a bell. Everyone rises and drinks to the heart.
I call the bar my heart and drink to that woman
in the corner. Here's to the heart, to that soak
of darkness starred by lust. Here's to all the hopeless
lovers in the world walking around knocked out.

—•—•—•—

Light Sips on Nothingness

It's always been like this:
a man leaves his family for one night out
though the weight he feels on his back
as he closes the door on his wife's embrace
is the hill the house once stood on.
So the house teeters on the edge
and years later as he drives by the darkened,
rocking house with its squat look of revenge,
he throws thoughts of the children out at them.

What is her pride if not the taking of revenge?
So she moves slowly through the things she left
unsaid and makes sure she'll never say them.
And if the evenings seem longer eating alone
she makes them longer by thinking everything
is over, that the empty bed in the mirror
is not the picture of a bed, but the reflection
of a blessing. There'll be no more second thoughts
of her standing in the mirror dressed to kill.

The questions children ask go clean through the heart,
arc around the world and go clean through again.
They want to know. Tell us why you're apart.
They stand there with your eyes as full authority.
The secret they hold is a shout. Love in the darkest
moment of a child's heart is simply light sleeping
with the lights on. They take aim by opening the heart.

—•—•—•—

Being Alive

You wake one morning, and the summer is dead,
but your eyes are still dazed by the tumultuous light
of yesterday, and in your ears you hear the roar of the sun
turned to blood. The color of the world has changed.

— Cesare Pavese

The small boy in the third row near the end
of the classroom wishes the future would arrive.
He feels keenly how it is to be someone, as he
heads over to the old man's variety store, certain
that someday he'll whistle down with both feet
inside a new man. The tune he whistles is a light
accompaniment to the history of the world.

The old man in the variety store is going blind.
He's waiting for some child to reach up to him
while the clouds that pass across his face bury him
in whiteness. Then he'll give out the wax lips and
mustaches so the little boy he's losing sight of
can run off wearing the expression of the immortals.

The small boy knows it takes an old man's strength
to hold down an empty street, that one slow shake
of an old man's head can erase a little boy. If only
the boy could change like the clouds, he could keep
the whiteness the old man sees before him. He tries
hard closing his eyes to make something of that darkness

inside him. He only feels how it is to be alive.
One day the old man stops in front of the school
to feel the sidelong glance of the afternoon light
weave in his glossy darkness the sweet smell of wax.
He listens with the stone posture of the turtle
to something so large it can't be heard. The old man,
light as a cloud, lets go of his love that tears off
like a land mass and passes through the air like air.
It makes the small boy look up to see who he'll become.

— • — • — • —

Call to be Left in the Air

My sons sleep in a house without a father.
I sleep without my sons.
When I ask myself What's this like?
I lose my balance.
I sleep without my sons.

Magnified in their dreams of me
coming closer, coming home, I hear voices
roaring and I'm on the phone:
"Hello, this is your father,

I saw on TV they shaved the horns of a bull today,
which could feel the shadow of a man passing by.
The bull was blunted, lost direction,
ended up stumbling through a sword."

"Is there any message, father?"
"Yes. There's an enormity of darkness
out here. Tunnels thin as wire
I can't get through."

I'm charging toward what I have to do,
this month receiving mail of skulls on fire,
tiny stick figures from Valhalla, saying, "To Dad!"
Perennial Halloween.

All my life I've been coming home.
But that's another story.
It has nothing to do with you,
sleeping in a house without a father,
me, sleeping without my sons.
Whatever it is, it's begun.

—•—•—•—

Another Coil

for that one who dropped dead in his tracks when he asked
and nobody answered

— Vincente Aleixandre

I have lived up here for two months now and know no one.
That window across the way from mine is my sun.
I think someone over there must also look at himself.

Today I can hear his dull yellow wall hand up the message
"No," as if bending back like this I were a question.
When I was a boy I thought I could walk through walls.

Sometimes it pleases me to stand on the balcony undressed
and listen to the hum of the voltage towers in the fog.
I get quietly thrilled under the mild, cold moon.

Then I go inside and hear a door slam. Someone's home.
Then from somewhere the cooking smells of soups and meats
open up my childhood days and, waking, I feel glad.

After days my woman knocks and for an instant I can't see her.
There's so much noise and light I hold her as if something
terrible had happened in the middle of a very nice day.

She tells me I'm sighing again. I'm sorry. I must allow myself
these long oar pulls across the room. It's not because of her.
It's almost not me. It's as if an old man weaving blue rope
inside me had told me he's finished with another coil.

—•—•—•—

Mockingbird, Copy This

Mockingbird, I've been working hard
on a small routine,
a series of one-liners,
a word meant to keep me going,
please keep me going,
toward what I am.

I heard your woman sort of moan
behind your song.
But it's a job isn't it,
the same old song
that God performed
when he made himself appear:
I Am Who Am.

Some God. Delusions of grandeur,
dissatisfactions, loneliness
that keeps us changing
a rivulet of wishes
into a river, a world,
the same old song.

Mockingbird, I don't know how you sleep.
I imagine you just hang on,
eyes wide open,
until the first star appears
then you sleep in its billion
blinking echoes.

I won't ask if you're happy.
Don't ask me.
But there's such a thing
as courage.
It's in your gaiety,
That's what I listen to.
Then sing.

—•—•—•—

Knock Turn

Everything's important and nothing matters.
That's how I learned to be a man, years of
hanging out in the streets, learning how to
stand and take it, give it, get it back.

Each night we'd go for something big and crazy
at the wide end of experience, so we'd have something
famous to talk about, make the sun shine off our teeth.

I woke up damaged from that sleep
and found that people don't even have the kindness
to say, I know what you mean. I'm no fool.
You know what I mean.

Tonight the summery sounds of punches and shouts
rise again from the darkened golf course of my childhood, and again I'm
kicking at the chest of what is now
the town undertaker. My God, the undertaker,
whose name was Bill. He knew he'd have another chance
to lay me out.

Back then I used to sit in a little black tree loaded
with ripe cherries and just close my eyes.
All I heard was bells. That's how I learned
a hundred kinds of silence can take the place
of things not done.

It was important pretending nothing mattered,
killing time at the height of a scream
where everyone wins and nothing is won.
Now I treat myself like a son.

—•—•—•—

Something Else

In this small room I'm beginning to feel
as if I'm being hunted down.
The mirror has doubled the size
of the opposite wall which goes on
forever saying nothing that refreshes me.

But, let's see, what pleasure did I memorize today?
The glance some beautiful woman gave me
was a gift. There are so many beautiful faces.
I always think each one must be thinking
some wonderful thing.

Yesterday I saw a wild composer play Ravel
with two different shoes on,
stepping on stars, stepping on wind.
I attribute his passionate performance
to absentmindedness, which I've got.

Just because I don't care what I look like today
in this city of beautiful faces,
anything seems possible. I could fly,
tunnel, walk, or remain seated.
I can go out or stay in.

Only sometimes I get so hungry for a woman
that I'll sit in a public place. I must look
desperate because even dogs stop sniffing me
and veer away. I wonder what could desperation
smell like until I enter my room.

I remember once I lived without desire. Now I wake
with fistfuls of silk and am astonished
it's just a trick of light. My desire
is no bigger than a pinpoint of light
in the eyes, yet it floods the world.

Now more than ever my life seems just
a sublimation of something else.
I could follow the dark splashes of desire
all the way down to their names
and still never get there, still never get to it,
never give up.

Tonight I'll wander like a love-struck boy
leashed by desire. The stars have come out
like beautiful prospects, faces in a doorway.
The coiled power of living alone is in me
and anything can happen. Anything will.

—•—•—•—

On Nights Like This

On nights like this I'm happy
simply being still.
It's a small happiness
like my mother's hand
brushing back my hair.
Even a child's peace of mind
can seem enormous.

When I was a boy I loved to stare
into the velvet-lined cases
of accordions and guitars.
Something that contains music
feels deeper than music,
darker than all the instruments
I threw away.

That left me by myself
wishing the wind would tear
layer after layer of me
in someone's direction. And I admit once
I tried to throw myself away.

But tonight I'm finding it
in my heart to forgive myself.
God knows why.
I lift the darkness, step inside,
and imagine the sun
hour after hour
slowly brush across the sky
until it's empty.

It's such a small happiness,
so much has passed,
I hold both hands.

—•—•—•—

Telepathic Note to Poet Friends

Friends, I'm lonely today.
Nothing's broken, only today I have no bones
and this softness needs an escort to its death.
So I'm watching the slow tarantellas of the snowflakes
wink and go out, thinking you've been crushed by less.

Lately I've admired the classic themes
of western movies: silence, practice, and space.
Each of us has waited for *it* to happen,
no matter what. It doesn't matter what.
It all comes down to facing a gun
and trying to say it while the sun fires away,
the horses melt, and next door a woman shrieks
a perfect poem at her kids. In other words,

we've all spent years in rooms snowing darkness,
packing it into the shapes of music, or maybe lovers.
So somewhere far off I hear a black piano resound
in sympathy. All I wanted to say, my friends, is
I'm amazed that you're still singing.

—•—•—•—

from

As Long As You're Happy

(1986)

Something Solid

First thing in the morning
I open my eyes,
look into the mirror
of my old armoire,
a bald man in stolen hospital pajamas
expecting to see
a distinguished man of letters,
like when the wine steward
stands over you
and expects you to decide
if what's in your mouth
meets the test
of whether the last ten years
in darkness
were good or not,

only this time
the door is open
and I'm staring incomprehensibly at five shelves
glutted with colored clothes:
"Wow, it's like looking inside my head!"
And then I think with these rags-for-brains
like the Straw Man does in Oz
about the whole idea of wearing clothes
and how beautifully my wife gets dressed
and how petty bourgeoisie materialism
turns out to be pretty smart,

when about this time
Mr. Pernell, retired oilman and rancher,
marches by the house on his morning exercise
with his wife walking ten yards behind him
as if they don't know each other
and he's thinking to himself,
"This is Professor Myers' house,"
and he's feeling good about the neighborhood
whose citizens, like me, he thinks,
have achieved something solid.

— • • —

Arf

Dogs give commands to me in one syllable,
the same one again and again.
I speak back in polysyllabics
above my one great bark.

It's like my dreams falling all night
in technicolor splendor. I can't remember what.
When I open my eyes and look back
I'm just grateful I fit my body through
this space as big as a bark.

And the conversations I have with myself each day. . . .
They're like those silver bells on poles
across which gags of burnt electricity arc.
And I'm laid out below, inert,
until my head smokes and I stagger off
with a grunt-thought, cough-out, my smashed send-off.

The same thing happened to my friend Larry
who claims he never woke up at birth.
So for $45 the holistic doctor placed a
bouillon cube of beef on his forehead and a lump
of cheese over his heart, and Larry woke up
and coughed and coughed in dog language
and we knew to bring him water! It was a miracle!
Only we're not sure what.

I imagine that's why we have the public flasher
who is able to prepare us
for the right moment on some random day
when he'll drop the blinding light of his body
down in front of us: "Bark!"
He makes us feel exact.

My intuition tells me yes
even a stone can bark.
Only the sound it makes is millions of years long
and I'm standing in the silence and dark
between its two great phonemes of need,
going to sleep, waking up, going to sleep.

— • • •

Do You Know What I Mean?

For the sake of argument
let's say there are three of me:
the one with the bummed-out body,
the one who senses things are going badly,
and the bright one who can't cope. That's me!
Don't get me wrong. It's a family.
For example, if #2 has a sexy dream,
#1 may salivate. That leaves 3 free to feel guilty
or write. Only sometimes in the face of authority
1 opens his mouth and 3 slips out "I hate your guts!"
Then 2 tries to get 3 to repent, but isn't smart enough
and then everyone feels like shit and gets a headache.

Do you know what I mean?

2 and 3 are always sniffing each other suspiciously
while 1 sticks a bottle of sour mash in his face.
We know that somewhere some elegant in a gray silk suit
and shiny black shoes reflecting the tips of the Alps
is slowly turning toward his tasty companion
the date 1957 on their green bottle of *pouille-fuisse*.

I did that so #3 would feel better
having said a spot of French.
That means 1 has the green light to celebrate
and 2 can slink around pretending he's French.

 *

Dear God,
I'm not sure I believe in you,
but #2 is feeling bad today.
He thinks you're out there and you're great.
But he can't tell the difference between something small
tearing apart and the sound of something large in the distance
moving far off.

So this is for my brother, #2,
standing here like we're in church.
Sometimes when we're quiet like this
I think we're all the family we've got.

— • — • —

Headache

I tried to remember to buy aspirin and soap
but I only bought the aspirin.
I liked the way that worked, the way I made my choice
unbeknownst to me. It was clean, as if I knew something
way down deep.

Because what if I only bought the soap?
Then I'd be locked out of my head in pain
trying to reach my brain by transcendental meditation,
which only makes the pain more real.

On the other hand, what if I bought both,
which may be normal, but
what if I remembered everything?

No thanks, I want to know who's on first.
I want my mind made up even if it means
I don't feel normal, or I have to keep a list,
which reminds me

of my delivery bike old George Lynch stole
and then he sold it and I got fired and then
he moved away. He is no more to me
than the window of light shining on that apple seed.
Besides, I'd rather be right than clean,
the little prick.

—•—•—•—

Where I've Been

At last I am ready to report
how so much of my time
has been lost between
thinking and feeling
that seen from above

it must look like a river
cutting its way between
age and circumstance
leaving behind something wet
and abstract as the insides of a jewel.

How I came to accept this habit
after wiping these journeys out
like dirty thoughts, pronouncing myself
time after time as being lost
is a testament to whatever lies
beyond my will.

I can hardly look at anything
as complex and frightening
as the human face, its ability to imagine
moving inward
at such tremendous speeds
it outruns the Postmaster's fear
of having to read his jumbled horde of letters.

All this is to my shame, my chandelier
of egotism burning in an empty head.
I feel as archaic as a candelabrum
floating in outer space.
I have even stopped writing poetry
thinking a simple report will do.

—•—•—•—

Planting Stones

I picked up a 25-pound rock
walked into the ocean chest-high
then sat down.

I thought the flaws within
might float away
like splinters.

I thought of walking toward Europe
and bursting on the horizon
like a great idea.

In the end there was an acre
of wall-sized stones, each one
solid as a held breath,
each one a moment to myself.

——• • •——

Coming to the Surface

Sometimes you get tired of the dark, the humming,
the shimmering and echoes of others,
the whole long story that robs you of your life.

So you break into the world
of air and light
just to feel heavy and freezing,
which is a good release from thinking
but not a permanent cure.

Once in a while someone plunges by you
with his being combed back
into a scream of forgetfulness,
a command.

He's going the other way.

—•—•—•—

Synchronization

What was I thinking
when they allowed me to choose
from all the orchards of music
and I picked the accordion?

I was thinking of my fierce brother
falling through ice and blackness
trying to master the piano
while with only one finger I thought
I could make a piano rise from the sea.

What was I thinking
when I modeled my best moment after
a bird startled into flight?

I was thinking of the sky
lowered to my height
so I could fly at eye level.

What I wanted was both sides fused
like the face of a one-eyed Jack,
to go out in ermine and silk with a faceful
of triumphal bugles.

And if that brightened the air
and burned the tips of leaves a little,
well, that's life.

What I didn't want was to go out searching
for the usual spicule of insight.
All I wanted was to go out thinking
I did what I thought I said.

—•—•—•—

Poem against Good Health

I quit all my bad habits so I could grow old
and one day say something big enough
to climb into and close like a box.

That's how one year went up in smoke,
waiting for whatever I did smart
to harden into words
while the nothing behind me
and the nothing before me
marched forward in their place.

All my consciousness
focused on what was different
so I forgot the main thing
like when you spot a fly in the room
the whole room softens and disappears,

which is how I became what I wanted to change.

Now it's impossible even to be simple,
but I've added years to my life
which is as invisible as if it never existed
and everyone's so proud of me.

—•—•—

The Correspondence School Poetry Teacher Speaks on the Relationship between Life and Art

They send me poems
like gargantuan emeralds
crashed into my house,

huge sputters of
wetness and light.

I, who, according to the best of my knowledge,
may or may not
have my socks on,

who can't remember how to call home
in cases of emergency,
they send me poems.

I forget the reasons why this reminds me
that our heads are

so disproportionately large at birth,
but I'll share with you instead
my basic principle:

"If you're thirsty, think of sour pickles."
I even have a slogan for the heart:
"Redeem yourself. Wipe out memory!"

No memory, no life, no art.
I have worked my way back down
to exactly what I've become—

vicarious, the ideal reader.
As Uncle Irv who sold storm windows used to say
when he'd wake up from his nap on Sunday visits,
"What . . . ?"

—•—•—

Mom Did Marilyn, Dad Did Fred

We sat there, her tiny audience,
as she slunk downstairs, poured
into her sparkling blue gown,
kissing the red-hot air and singing
"Diamonds are a girl's best friend"
into each of our little faces
that blushed at how deeply she was
committed to being sexy, and at Dad
suavely twirling her out the house
and down the street in his convertible.

The tuna fish sandwiches, the blitzed TV
faded in an obliterating glitter
of glitz and wet kisses, and I
with my face turned toward
the heaven of things I would do someday
made up my mind too soon
to have other notions of beauty.

—•—•—•—

As Long As You're Happy

I don't know what the Bible says.
My mother who died after being
mercilessly kept alive
by machines at the hospital
looked at the photo of my fiancée
and said, "As long as you're happy . . ."
as if it were the final measure of my reach.

The star through which I shot
my young heart has little value now
except as an occasional reference point,
a piece of cosmic punctuation
some third-rate planet may depend on
to survive.

What I thought was an ethical problem
of existence was just a broken heart.
The woman for whom I have ransomed
my wife and children would like to erase
the past. I would like to gather them all,
please, under one roof, one heart.

About my mother . . .
each day the doctors and machines
said her chances of living
with one more operation
on her overburdened heart
would probably be better.
I thought of reading the Bible then.
It wasn't a question of being happy.

—•—•—•—

I Will Steal Some for Her from You

The way I hold you for dear life,
entwine your sleep with mine,
is the way my mother's letters say
she's fine and do not mention she is old,
that each eye has revolted from its axis
in her search for what is missing.

Her hug crushes
but cannot touch what's wrong.

I never bought you jewelry
because silver and turquoise spill
from your slightest question,
necklaces of laughter slide from the sides of the bed.
But someone has been paring and slicing,
grating and crumbling my mother's voice.

Whatever she is saying, the noise of miners
is roughing back the edge.

Once she had an assortment of pretty dresses
and men hungry for her. Now she has courage
and grown sons on whom she has worn herself out
like a washrag on the rocks.

Thinking of her stooped over,
I feel the world's been finally cleaned.

I tell you this because nobody has
explained it to me. Who would bother
to explain a letter rising on the wind?
But the hammer falling. . . .
There needs to be an explanation.

—•—•—•—

Leaving the Light On

Returning home late one night
I realized I had no idea
who Mother and Father were.
So I climbed our spindly apple tree
wondering why darkness made me larger
and peered inside their room
listening first to one,
then the other, like oars
dipping in the darkness
towing the lighted window away.

They were explaining while they spoke
the simple names of things
through which the world fell through
confused: Mother, Father, Home;
offering directions
to each other
like polite strangers,
the ones who go on
when it's all done,
half finished, just begun,
and they go on.

—•—•—•—

The Gift

Remember Father's Day, the banner says.
But I can't give my father what he wants
much less name it, so I get him a golf machine
that pops the ball right back.

If I can't give him what he wants
I can get him what seems wrong.
It's the thought that counts, he'd say,
not having caught the exact misses
I sent past him into interstellar space.

I'm telling my wife how she looks supergood
in this flouncy purple maternity suit,
though in truth it looks like her behind
is in front, when I suddenly think
I'm going to be a father! and I remember
my own two kids who don't live with me anymore
and I get quiet in order to receive their thoughts.

But instead I think about these poor Black kids
I took for a ride through White North Dallas
and how one little six-year-old beauty
leaned over my shoulder and shouted to the wind,
"How do you get to live like this?"

—•—•—•—

Imbalance

Just before leaving her room
I pull the curtain back and reveal
the wheeling universe that falls
over the house and will not stop falling.

She loves in the silent profusion
of young girls who give off the scent
of cinnamon and, busying the air with images,
she circles her nipples with her fingertips
then falls asleep.

It's impossible to be accurate
going by the feel of things.
The light of the star she singled out
to make a wish
was extinguished before her birth.

I work best with darkness and this is it,
the dark block of emptiness I live in,
from which no sound or light escapes.

I'm building an aesthetic
based on imbalance
as the Korean potters did
for a small off-kilter work.
It'll complement the Earth:
an enormous intention inside a small life.

I wonder what she wished.

—•—•—•—

The Diamond Explanation

In your braided hair
I have placed a diamond
like the small silence
we undress inside.

Love's beautiful nail
makes a stunning light remark
about pressure and darkness:
how long it takes, faced with myself,
to break open a little light.

Take this morning. Chained
to my cigarettes, I got toting
the instruments of my habit
thinking nothing of the accumulation
of ashes and smoke, which is
a terrible metaphor for love
that lovers understand.

They know the great thing about being human
is its depth, the thoughtlessness and art
of every gesture, the responsibility
of the still life left behind.

This is why I bought the diamond,
to remind me of the Everlasting
from blown ashes and smoke,
of solitude's wild and quiet transformations
while we're getting dressed.

—•—•—•—

A Manner of Speaking

My wife exclaimed, *¡Que macho!*
How mature your penmanship is!

I said, *That is nothing, my bird-like bird,*
but why do you speak to me in Spanish?

Oh, she said with her little mouth stuck like a cherry tomato,
reminding me of the time she had called me a jeweler with a salad,

I was to market today and this stallion of a farmer
took me in his arms and sold me muchas penumbras.

¡Que Dios, Conchita Estrellita con Quesa! I explained.
Do you think it is me when I am not at the market?

She twirled her entire lovely body around twice and said
in her palest voice, *No, Herbert, my life is the trudging bore*
I'm trapped inside of. I would soon evaporate in madness
if it weren't for the efficacious power of your vocabulary.

That is nothing, my flower-like tulip, I said, asking
if we were now in England and by what fortuitous trick
in my expression had we been transported there.

Mon Cher, she whispered, twisting her waist coquettishly,
reminding me of the sensual syntax of Balzac,

Zee chauffeur took me to a tiny garden on zee outskirts
of zee city—tres magnifique—and there in your name honor
praised your incomparable generosity to zee hilt.

Mon Dieu! I gasped, *Francois de Monde du Vichyssoise,*
is it me you think I am when I am not in the driver's seat?

Ziegfried, she shuddered, *vhen vill you see zee devastating*
power off your mind on me? Your mere presence eez incredible.

Zat eez noszing, my doe-like fawn, I laughed, to which
she laughed, and then my laughter roiled over hers, and then
she cut under mine, and then I tried my lower boiling gutterals,
and she careened even higher, and so I could do nothing but
enlarge the geography of our joy as she set sail and I
watched over her to discover, as it were, the farthest regions
of our communal bliss.

—•—•—•—

Natural Ice Cream

Sometimes when I'm tired of your dark beauty,
my right hand grows enormous,
the tunnel of my eye grows inward,
and I can't bear to eat a piece of fruit.

I love you, I love you, I love you with all my heart,
I say,
driving the car back and forth
over a pomegranate,
the rpm needle's stuck on red.

And now my brain outweighs me,
now I'm tired.
After I clean up the house
I'm gonna put a bullet through my head.

Later on, we can go out someplace nice
for natural ice cream.

—•—•—•—

The Diaspora

By what name will they call
the disheveled temple
inside me
except by my name?

In whatever city this is
whoever hears the congregation
of my voices chanting
in a rented room
will be disabled by them.

I keep two immaculate white cats
to restore my memory of tranquility
and I have nailed the people I love
in another life and more and more
the temple is inscribed
in an alphabet of indecipherable
accidents and impressions.

Once I looked up to a God who wore
an expression from a joke
I never quite got. Now I hide my face
in the beauty of my lover
whose cries of pleasure twist shamelessly
like smoke beneath a door.

She tells her father maybe someday
I'll be famous, but he thinks
it's only in the way
someone has perfected a technique
for decanting a dangerous fluid.

She puts the stone I'm curled inside of
in her mouth and speaks about our future
in which I am the distant blueness
and the blown stars of her breath
are lights along our way. I hold onto her
blinded by promises.

After the many deaths and accomplishments,
each of us makes an order of our own.
I think this solitude of rock
is a tiny piece of God's great loneliness

in which birds with strings of sunlight
in their beaks fly through. So the saying
of my name makes an order of its own.

—•—•—•—

Like Trees in the Desert

As if they were planting a garden of flesh
with rulers and sticks and hands and boots
they used to beat us hard in Hebrew School.

We were terrible kids, always raising our hands
to go to the bathroom, please, and always denied.
So once we did it in a paper bag, lit the bag on fire,

and roared when the teacher tried to stomp it out.
They beat us with the literal and we cried out
for God to hold those beatings in His hand and

strike the teacher dead. I always wandered off
in my head trying to figure out just whose body
I was in and what the hell is all this anyway?

I remember nothing of my childhood except its streets
and the way sharp stones jutted out, which means
I must've been looking down a lot. Oh, I remember paying

my dime each week to buy a tree in Israel, leaf by leaf,
to make the desert bloom. And I assume that by now
somewhere in the desert there's a tree representing me.

—•—•—•—

Now, Children, Close Your Books

They have bolted the swivel seats to the floor
and washed out the gaping mouth of the blackboard.

Dust from the moon hangs in the buzzing fluorescence,
the sound of children made to sit still.

The octogenarian crossing guard disappears into the distance
waving his orange flag at death, but only a few cars stop.

Now, Children, open your books
to the page where anything can happen:

If you are X and the dull hours of afternoon light
lifting the building a little bit are Y

and the rank smell of bologna and bread inside your desk
has the power to remind you of arithmetic thirty years later

and all teachers are old ladies dying
with the names of objects and flowers

and a haunting voice drives through you
and makes up your mind to never return

and that feeling you held
like a lucky penny in your hand

you can't name or find or live for anymore—
then, Children, how will you live?

—•—•—•—

Most of Us

In another age I would've married a sorry woman
from my small village, had too many children,
broken my back with my hands, and come home drunk.

I would've died early from diseases, having suffered
humiliation after humiliation, my heart twisting at the sight
of a coin, while our hated king lived far off on a hill.

I would've believed in anything that was given,
been on my knees to anything with a singular face.
I would not have been as I am, one who believes in himself

and nothing else, to whom everything else is in service,
and live up here in a bewilderment of choices,
doing what I choose, The King of Everything.

—•—•—•—

Contributor's Note

I am brushing what's left of my hair
beautifully, slowly
in honor of the year I froze in an unheated warehouse
and for my dog, Sam, who couldn't take it and took off.

While my father explained what I looked like
with the question, "How can you live like this?"
I thought the hard facts of life would build character.
I was in the big city on maneuvers, going through myself like war.

I am taking my time deciding which arm
should go into my worn shirt first
in memory of the people I squandered
with my eyes shut
to whom, for whatever kept them with me, I apologize,
and who, for whatever they saw in me that was good,
couldn't possibly know the vanishing point I believed in,
that there would hardly be room for myself.

In the old days I couldn't possibly make a mistake:
the cold, the hunger, the twisted nightpeople,
the useless jobs, in back rooms, basements, laboratories,
high-rise cubicles, dizzying ledges, open sea, lonely cab,
looking in the mouth of kegs of nails, the human brain,
shark guts, mock-ups; from a ten-story scaffold
to my tent on Bolinas Mesa, I look back
out of broken back and bridgework at the incredibly open
face in my high school yearbook which quotes me as saying,
"Do your best."

And it has come to this taking my time
to get ready, this stuffing my blood
with corsages of debris and neglect.
I am washing my face slowly because
the ceremony of slow deciding is itself
getting ready, and taking my time means
I am not ready, go on without me,
I am not ready yet.

——•—•—•——

Cross Country

I never woke you as we drove across
the Great Plains in the high darkness
trying to reach the Mississippi, me
listening so hard to a small metallic noise
inside the engine's roar that it seemed quiet
as I drove on tense, exhausted, undecided,
until you woke and heard me say go back to sleep.

I can still hear you shout "Get out!"
as the wheels fell off our marriage
and our son, sobbing and hugging our knees,
tried holding us together. Sometimes when I call
I close my eyes and follow that line
flying through the darkness like a Roman candle
ending in a burst of darkness and ringing,
and my own small voice out there on its own
comes back at me, asking "Hello, who is this, hello?"

—•—•—•—

Waiting for the Part with a Bite out of Me to Snap

I was used to hearing my neighbors cursing "Christ!"
and the walls of my house so thin
I thought someone's calling me
and I'd get up and say
"Okay, I'll fix it," and I'd end up
with my head inside the "everything drawer"
looking for my goddamned melted hammer
so I'd whack what was wrong back in place.
And when I fixed it so it didn't move
I'd say to myself like a one-trick dog,
"Pretty Good, have a beer."

In those days it was almost always winter
and the sweet old hungers drove me inward
and I'd trudge upstairs and pull the chain
to light the darkness up, and then I'd write
while the vines grew crazily across the window
and the cats sat waiting to beam me down.

In those days everything was going to happen
because I said so, and a promise was a promise,
because I knew I knew a few things deep enough
so when I'd say these things I'd never blink:
"Once and for all, this is for keeps."

And eventually I got across. Everything's finally fixed.
I've got a garden full of pecans and plums and a skyful
of passing pleasantries. Lying here, I imagine painting
a courtesan in a purple sari through which the afternoon light
is shining. And she, feeding me fruits and nuts, is giving
herself to me bit by bit under the guardian trees
against a harmony of blue.

But then there's the feeling of a specific lack of depth
and I suggest right out of the blue there should be
a strike force of stony blackbirds
diving diagonally down.

—•—•—•—

from

Blindsided

(1993)

Jake Addresses the World from the Garden

Rocks without ch'i [spirit] are dead rocks.
—Mai-Mai Sze, *The Way of Chinese Painting*

It's spring and Jake toddles to the garden
as the sun wobbles up clean and iridescent.

He points to the stones asleep and says, "M'mba,"
I guess for the sound they make, takes another step

and says, "M'mba," for the small red berries crying
in the holly. "M'mba" for the first sweet sadness

of the purplish-black berries in the drooping monkey grass,
and "M'mba" for the little witches' faces bursting into blossom.

That's what it's like being shorter than the primary colors,
being deafened by humming stones while the whole world billows

behind the curtain, "M'mba," the one word. Meanwhile I go on
troweling, slavering the world with language as Jake squeals

like a held bird and begins lallating to me in tongues.
I follow him around as he tries to thread the shine off a stone

through the eye of a watchful bird. After a year of banging
his head, all the crying, the awful falling down, now he's trying

to explain the vast brightening in his brain by saying "M'mba"
to me again and again. And though I follow with the sadness

above which a stone cannot lift itself, I wink and say
"M'mba" back to him. But I don't mean it.

— • • •—

Visitation Rites

—for my son Seth

My gentle son is performing tricks for me on his bicycle.
He's fourteen and has just cracked open the storm door
to manhood with his gently lowered voice shredding
into shadows until he's surrounded by the calls of
tan young girls whose smooth brown skin calls out, "We're alone."

It will not be long before he masters standing still
on one wheel, elegant jumps over obstacles, riding
upside down and backward until he will have made
of danger a pretty colored bird to delight him,
sending it away, calling it home, calling it home
as it sails and grows larger, darkens and adds weight.

I watch how well he'd done without me all these years,
me with my iron sled of guilt, my cooked-out piles of
worry smoldering. I have been his only model, he says,
and shares with me what a typical day of winning is like.
I sit on a little hill watching my son show off his
light dominion over gravity, knowing in the next few minutes

I will leave again for another year, and again our lives
will pull apart and heal over like bubbles separating in two.
This is how he says good-bye—without speech or reasons or
the long looking after that I've honed through time—
just a flash in the sun he's suddenly perfected, and I'm gone.

—•—•—•—

Have a Nice Day

No, no, I don't want my heart broken again today.
I don't want to hear the slosh and slide of another country-
western tune about bars and broken-down love and junky pickups,
though they're more than real enough. And I don't want to feel
the sentimental night sweats rising up from someone's childhood,
or tangle with the slashes of abstract art drying in the track-lit air
of grown-up feelings, watching the colors of memory and fact intersect
and crash like trucks, as if thought were feeling, and feelings, trucks.

I just want what we used to wish for in the 1950s, to have
"a nice day," back when a woman would seriously ask without blinking,
"If I take off all my clothes, will you take care of me the rest of my life?"
Back when most of the guys I knew would've given this serious thought,
though it all seems sort of silly now, almost heartbreakingly incompetent
in its innocence, in its presumption of real loss, like the guys
elbowing each other on the corner, asking "How far did you get?" as if
the body, like the expression "nice," were a place you could retire to.

Everyone's suffered real losses, which means there is no "far enough."
And I don't want to harken back to yesteryear when being good or bad
was the simple difference between an open heart (now a surgical procedure)
and a closed door (signifying power), back when work was poetically called
"earning a living," as if merely living weren't work enough.
Everyone seems headed for his own compulsory heart attack, proving, yes,
the heart has gone far enough. And I'm not sure what's coming next

though yesterday I saw some kids with Day-Glo hair and death heads
on their teeth. They were sloppily slam-dancing on ice, which was just
their way of probably saying yes, we're broken-hearted, without taking
their clothes off. That seems more than hard enough. Today I just want
to relax, bring my blood pressure down to the level of rush-hour traffic.
I suppose that makes me as outdated as this tree I'm sitting under,
on whose every leaf is a black-eyed, green-bellied cicada buzz-sawing
its wire-and-cellophane grade-school wings in the last-chance blood lust
of August. They seem willing and able to leave the burning husks
of their bodies behind in the trees, as I seem to be doing
for the sake of a kind word.

—•—•—

Not Thinking of Himself

—for Mark Cox

"Today," he said to the mirror, "the person I am inside of
will not be allowed to think of himself. Not once!"

And immediately he smashed his toe on the corner of the sink
but thought only of his mother who used to pinch his cheeks
like this—"Ow!"—and crush his chest like that—"Ow!"

He wondered briefly if under his rules it would be allowable
to do something nice for someone such as himself
who didn't know he existed.

And immediately he stood up and banged his head on the water tank
but thought only of his father who used to hit him on the head
like this—"Ow!"—and punch him in the stomach like that—"Ow!"

It was then that he thought of his life as an inside-out sock,
and wondered briefly if calling himself by another name completely
might give him a bigger head start.

—•—•—•—

The Experts

When the man in the window seat
flying next to me
asks me who I am
and I tell him I'm a poet,
he turns embarrassed toward the sun.
The woman on the other side of me
pipes up she's four-foot-ten and is going to sue
whoever made these seats.

And so it is I'm reminded how I wish I were
one of the aesthetes
floating down double-lit canals
of quiet listening, the ones
who come to know something as
mysterious and useless
as when a tree has decided to sleep.

You would think for them
pain lights up the edges of everything,
burns right through the center of every leaf,
but I've seen them strolling around,
their faces glistening with the sort of peace
only sleep can polish babies with.

And so when a waitress in San Antonio
asks me what I do, and I think
how the one small thing I've learned
seems more complex the more I think of it,
how the joys of it have overpowered me
long after I don't understand,

I tell her "Corned beef on rye, a side of salad,
hold the pickle, I'm a poet," and she stops to talk
about her little son who, she says, can hurt himself
even when he's sitting still. I tell her
there's a poem in that, and she repeats
"Hold the pickle, I'm a poet,"
then looks at me and says, "I know."

— • • • —

How?

The fat lady behind the counter at the gas station
wore a pin that said, "I've lost 15 lbs. Ask me how!"
That was answered by the vision of her daughter,
obviously being punished, bent over a book in the corner,
like a Vermeer painting, only reversed.

Then it struck me how that girl, quietly displayed there,
was like her mother's button, and I wanted to ask her how.
But her mother snapped a few bills into my extended hand,
saying, "Have a nice day," meaning, mind my own business.

I guess I half-expected the daughter to flash me a desperate look,
like in the movies where the mirror in the ladies' room
is scrawled in blood, "I've lost 15 lbs. Ask me how!"
But she never gave me the slightest look.

And as I pounded the car across the compressor hose, I knew that
in the movie I would've leapt from the swerving car and crashed
headfirst through the complacency of their plate glass window
where they pretended to be the perfect picture of the average

alienated American family, with Dad out back under a car,
and I'd put a gun to her fat mother's head and nonchalantly say,
"Okay, Baby Cups, unless you want to lose another 15 lbs.,
you better tell me how, and tell it to me slowly."

Only in real life I just drove on
swerving toward the "before picture" of the daughter,
surprised at how far out of myself I had gone,
blindsided by the "after picture" of her mother,
who pinned me under the wreckage of some incomprehensible sadness,
making me check and recheck my change.

—•—•—•—

The Wild and Real Agency

Once I took my wife against her will
to a modeling studio, helped her change
into dozens of compelling women, took her
down the long corridor of self-doubt
to a flood-lit room where she stood alone
against a pulled-down sky of blue.

The owner, who was secretly going out of business,
kept urging the ultimate woman out of her,
the way rock stars struggle toward their scream:
"Lemme have a little more. More pout. I need
that sadness, Baby. Now lemme have more leg."

That interested me when we first got married,
the dance behind the dance, but "The last thing
that is coming out of me," she said, "is me."
"Perfect, Babe," he said looking at her upside down
from beneath his black hood, and the flashbulbs
went off like fast days passing.

Then a real model came in complaining about her work.
She made this business of phony pleasure an object of belief,
and we felt foolish, my wife half-undressed, and me
caught with the next change of costume frozen in my head.

I guess it was that sense of cheapness and the opportunity
to escape that created an aura of beautiful importance between us,
like lovers in foreign films, as if the heart
had gained its final coup through an ordinary distraction,
or maybe Beauty herself decided it was time to show us her

surreal leg. "Who goes to a mall to be famous?" my wife said
as we drove home with the windows down, thrilled there was
real weather, taking the curves in slowly, and my wife
stretched back in her faded jeans looking really beautiful.

—•—•—•—

Why Don't You Ask Your Father?

> *Action is so epigrammatic, discharging its meaning like a joke.*
> *Every deed is a loss of consciousness; every act is a*
> *black-out.*
>
> —John Hollander, "Translation from the French"

After I bought our little kiddie pool and set it up,
I realized I had placed it under an overhang without a gutter,
and, of course, the weatherman called for rain. And so
I scrounged around the house for stuff to make a cover

and, for height, I used our old director's chairs,
the ones we sit in when we argue, which we got for showing up
at a time-share place in Arkansas and announced on cue,
"We only want the gift!"

Then to smooth that out I placed a plastic laundry basket
upside down on top of them, the one that wrenched my back
just before my fatal trip to meet your mother who laid me out
all week in her guest room for the dead, and then

I jerry-rigged my painter's tarp across that, the one
that I salvaged from my one and only business, and stretched it
taut across some wires I broke off from the tomato cages,
in which you mistakenly grew decorative pickle dwarfs,

and fitted them together with some duct tape I had borrowed
from my neighbor who has five kids and no hope and no job
and then placed the fragile top across the tottering platform
of the laundry basket and then carefully sliced open

our old prenuptial waterbed, which was always cold and
rolly anyway, and plunked that down on top of everything
so it wouldn't all blow away, and then I built a runway
from the garden timbers I ripped off from the railroad yard

where we had our first romantic encounter and ran those suckers
straight out across the yard and under the fence and out to
the city gutter. I've found that like me everything has
a use opposite to its intended. And then I slammed on

my old Nor'easter hat and matching yellow slicker,
which I kept from my fiscally pitiful lobstering days,
and with my kids jumping up and down crying "Daddy! Daddy!"
in the window, I sat there by the pool waiting for the
rain—it goddamn better rain—to come.

◆ ◆ ◆

The Amazing Obsolete TV Magnifying Viewer

What a disappointment, like looking through the end of a Coke bottle
at *The Ed Sullivan Show*, its lurid edges glowing all the way
to the spare bedroom where Aunt Jenny, once the class act of the family
in her svelte black dresses and gold jewelry, now blind in one eye
from hardening of the arteries, sat wheezing on the edge of the bed
from emphysema in her blowsy bathrobe and pink bunny slippers,
examining the identical cleaved halves of her migraine headache.

In those days the juggling acts always seemed so stupid,
whole extended families of Slavs brought in for a command performance:
mothers, fathers, uncles, children all standing on top of each other's
shoulders, all rocking madly on a teeter-totter board
to the music of the Russian kazatsky, while torches and swords
flew like family arguments up and down the human ladder.

I had just turned thirteen and was the family's self-appointed critic.
I sat a room away sniping at the rotten talent while the family,
without looking back at me, dismissed my running commentary
with an exasperated, "Oh, Jackie!" meaning I couldn't spot a metaphor
if it were burned onto a stage with sweeping spotlights.

And it was true. All I was doing was erasing the past as it ran,
though it all seems sharp as a subpoena, with me the hostile witness
screaming offstage, "Heresay! Heresay!" while the family flickered,
disbanded, some going mad, the rest "dying from fatal diseases."

All the while things in my head kept getting blurrier and bigger,
like the amazing obsolete TV magnifying viewer whose dot of light
diminished as I forgot it all—the house with its furor and heartaches
demolished, and me, still sitting there in the formal living room,
a room away, watching the family amazed at the juggling acts,
ooing and ahhing, and me, waiting to grow up, just waiting.

— • — • —

Attack of the Killer Power Tools

The whine of a circular saw
flew around the house today
like the prehistoric mating call
of some zinc-voiced mutant insect.
It came cornering this way,
clean as a right angle
spewing a snowstorm of decisions
I just couldn't put my finger on.

I felt like the studio violinist
who stayed home practicing
his entire childhood,
sawing his way through
facsimiles of the classics,
and turned out to be
a studio violinist.

So I painted the kitchen cabinets
with what turned out to be
a garish semi-gloss blue
like the horses on the merry-go-round
rearing up from what I took to be
a relentless electrical shock
while the world went round and round.

That's when my wife came in screaming
Stop this kitchen now!
which slowed my enthusiasm down
to a thousand-pound vowel,
which felt like I was standing
on my own sad song
about the little bald man
in the fluorescent hardware store
vowing to me this color was
true Renaissance blue.

I felt as if I had been holding a violin
under my chin for years, which reminded me
of my appointment at the dentist
who lectures me until my mouth is numb
though he lets me put the pedal of his drill
to the floor while he goes over and over

the smallest details until I feel at home
inside the bad art on his wall.

All this practicing of distractions
and crossed-out mistakes makes me think
I could be the Jackson Pollock of my life,
and I could scribble that out too,
if I had a mind to.
Only once in a while I stand back
from my life and think
there must be a power tool for this.

———•—•—•———

Vanishing Days

When I was a child
I ran and leapt along the beach
until I was made of
the striking power of wind.

I swam out and dove beneath
the cold blue water
and did somersaults
until I felt beautiful like water.

And when I wrote, first I lost
my right hand, then both arms,
and when I came to an understanding
only a ring spread out where I was.

I suppose I will go on doing this
to feel the impossibly huge things
of this world pass through me
as if I were missing. To live fully,
I had to have a perfect disguise.

—•—•—•—

Sometimes, Sweetie, You Think Too Much

When he wanted to tell her
something important,
he'd get a big feeling
like a dumpster being lifted
over the front of his face.

And just as he was about to
unload, she'd say something
little-and-sweet and beside-the-point
and he'd end up in a fit
of random air brakes.

When he'd wake up in the morning
looking like he just came home from work,
he'd intone, "I have a terrible grief to tell, . . ."

and she'd look into the faces of
her chipped toenails and sort of
half warn, half sing,
"Oh, hootie, tootie, mootie, smootie, rootie . . ."

—•—•—•—

Washed Up

When the flyweight
who was just a skinny kid
with the snappy moniker,
La Cucaracha, went down
in the first round
from a short right cross
my sister could've taken,
it was pretty obvious
he didn't want to box.
He wanted out.
He just sat there
busted up, twice defeated
in two pro fights,
his pipe-stem arms
dangling through the ropes,
his head slung down
as if he were enduring
another hellish argument
at home, the gulps of light
from hungry reporters
ripping into him
like his father
screaming, *Get a job!*

It was funny at first
seeing him sink down,
legs splayed like a girl's,
like your little sister's,
counting her defeat
her best escape.
Then it was sad
'cause you could see
he didn't have the heart,
that he was only waiting
for someone to help him up,
tell him, *It's okay, kid, go home.*
Then it was kind of quiet,
kind of scary as we began to relate,
like watching the dead
grow hair and nails,
and still no one came.

Oh well, we thought,
trying to change the subject,
what's next?
But the camera stayed on him,
coldly telling us
what to think,
while the kid couldn't
figure out how to get
his mouthpiece out.
It was as if he had discovered
some huge foreign thing
in his mouth, like in the
beginning of a horror movie,
when his hand couldn't grasp
this glistening red mass,
couldn't gasp or cough it up.
What's next? we wondered,
gently turning to one another
as men seldom do, our minds
flexed for the punchline
of a joke.
But when we turned back
the kid was gone
and somebody's sister
was flung over the hood
of a new red sports car
and that was that.

And I forgot about the kid
until this morning
when I was watching a
dingy gray seagull
walking along, poking at the
receding shoreline and thinking
how stupid it is
just to settle for whatever
is accidentally washed up
when there's millions of square miles
of ocean lying unconscious
next to him, if he'd just lift his head.
The whole thing seemed like
some huge and subtle screening process
I just couldn't figure out,

like someone who's been
on the road too long,
tired of not being in control
of where or when he sleeps,

like coming out of a movie
into the roaring light of a day
you had forgotten
and being faced with
seeing everything finally
for what it is. I don't know—
the sea, the fight, the clichéd
story of his life—
maybe it was just a case of
selective perception
and later on
inside some woman that night
he'd pull out and it'd all seem
like a case of mistaken identity.

I don't know,
I used to like the fights,
the edgy waiting, the thrill
of knocking someone out,
the fists, the muscle, the shouts.
Now I mostly hear the body punches
slamming home, the twisting of the
turnbuckles. All of a sudden
I feel what it's like
to be hooked in the mouth
and pulled up into a life
not your own,
the kid with a name
that doesn't fit,
beaten up, craning his neck around
to see what he's missed,
getting to his knees,
confused and humiliated,
swearing he can keep on
taking it
if that's what they want,
if that's what it takes,
if that's it.

The Energy It Takes to Pass through Solid Objects

— for my son Jacob

My son with food on his face
is banging on his high chair like a prisoner
who has lost the ability to speak.

He would like to grab the cat
who has slipped by like the field mouse
fleeing her mind. His demands rise and disperse
like night rising off the skull of morning.

Last night we let him sleep between us
and he thrashed around wrestling sorrows
his own size. Then he sat up quietly
in the dark like a miniature alien,
my own exposed heart, calmly weighing
the critical mass of stillness between us.

My son with food on his face,
food oozing through his fists,
screams his life is like no other.
He is being pulled straight out of his chair
by the long black fur of his imagination
and all I can do, he screams, is nothing.

I try to remember but I can't sing
the song my mother sang to me
that made a solid object out of feeling.
I open my mouth and with the energy it takes
to pass through solid objects, I arrive silently
at that place from which all feeling comes.

It will take a long time to make him civil,
before we can unstrap him from the raucous
taste of peas and screaming orange carrots,
and let him leave this house. He will have to loop
on wider and wider journeys, joining his circle
to ours, until the food he orders is exotic,
and inside the elusive feel of soft black fur
is the woman he will marry and the raggle-taggle
parade of cats and family.

He cries and his cries float up, joining ours,
the ones we don't notice. So I show my son the rain
and he shrieks and shrieks delightedly.
This is how it is for him all day—
rain from one moment to the next, all day
falling down through wet exclamation points.

There is no toy for this. Only sleep.
And so I stay with him caught halfway in-between
the desire to be someone else and his stuffed animal,
mouth sewn shut, eyes pasted wide open, arms flung out.

———•—•—•———

The Stopover

Just as he was falling asleep, the phone rang.
It was from a distant relative who had just "deplaned."
That word made it official, case closed, nothing could be done.

He looked up to heaven at his people from The Old Country
who wearily lifted their heads from shoveling six feet of snow
off the potato farm and asked as more snow fell,
"Has the time finally come when things have gone from bad to worse?"

Well, if she wanted to come, whoever she was,
then fine, she could come.
If it would bring a little happiness
into this sorry world,
then fine, let her come.

But first, business was bad.
And next, there was the shock
of going bald all at once.
And then there was a lifetime of
dwelling on death,
And now—what else?—this!
This just wasn't a good time for a visit.

—•—•—•—

A Living

— for Jerry Stern

Jerry, you would've loved my grandmother's backyard.
Crabgrass, stickers, sand, rhubarb, and garbage cans
out of which leapt the Lords of Monday Morning—radiant
dog-size rats that I can still feel frisking the old
two-decker house from its stone-walled cellar
to its thin stink of whitefish in the upstairs kitchen.

We had a glowering skyline of houses back then that answered
the sea like Pop did the door: "Goddammit, who is it!?"
No lifeguards or pastel condos, just waterfront property
like the kind you find on the Ganges, and pious old Jews
like Gramma Belle sitting in her picture window in a haze
of smoke and steaming coffee, staring at the waves of by-gone years.

In those days no one got raped or robbed. The trend back then
was to drop dead in Miami, smelling of arguments, chicken soup,
and broken hallways. Am I coming through? All skin and bones
in my cheap gabardines? Like we used to answer the question,
"So how are you?" with the question, "So how should I be?"

I wasn't going to be another skinny Ashkenazi half dead on the beach
from third-degree burns with a dumb newspaper boat on my head, afraid
of a heart attack in knee-deep water. So I stayed in the backyard
in the exotic green break of rhubarb, cracking a stalk in half,
sucking on the sour juice—Mr. Romance, who would one day score.

This morning my eyes are sore and there's a dark line down my cheek
like a near-death experience from a cello slide by Mahler.
I'm in my robe with its coffee stain like a monogram of my unconscious,
smoking, drinking coffee, walking to my classes at the university
to teach poetry, which can explain almost everything, and happens to be,
should someone like the landlord ask, a living.

—•—•—•—

Supersaver to Atlanta

Sitting next to me was a young Black carpenter
who at the end of the trip, after several drinks
and nervous swappings of disorders and near disasters,
gently entrusted his name to me, "David."
Looking away, he told me about his six-year-old son
who didn't know his colors. "It hurt me," he said,
holding his hand against his heart, patting it,
then pointing at the sky full of continuing blue,
"that he'd look at this and guess it was red."
I felt bad for him, but thought that seeing blue
and saying red pointed to something basically true
about being human.

"Where's he now?" I asked, fearing the worst,
flustered, as if I had spilled my drink in my lap.
"He's with his mother," he said, "I took him from my girl
who's too busy trying to look pretty for her men."
I asked if he were married and, without a trace of guilt,
he said, "No, she's got other kids by different men.
You got to put in time with kids. You got to pay
attention," he said, cupping his face against the window
so he could get a clearer view of what we were flying through.

He looked no older than my firstborn son
who lives away from me. He had a dark sweet face
but made sure he talked practical. Behind us
a squawky stewardess with a heavy Southern twang
kept going over and over the words "right" and "left"
in Spanish: "*Derecho. Derecho. A la izquierda.*" I thought
she had her genders switched but couldn't remember,
then realized she was practicing for a crash
and I settled on trying to memorize the exits.

Then he asked me if I'd like to play his *Word Games* book,
and I regret to say I told him I taught college English.
"Uh-huh, that's nice," he said, "that's nice. . . ."
Then he opened up the book to the puzzle of *Cinderella*
whose camouflaged words ran forward, backward,
up and down, and obliquely within its square.
They were all there: *evening, sad, stepmother, prince,*
the story of the girl who suffered others' words
but paid attention and got her wish. Then I realized

if I just looked at the puzzle as if I were listening
to each individual instrument in a symphony all at once,
and honed in on the long horns floating in the middle,
that I could easily spot the word. I opened my mind
and thought of Dick Hugo, the poet-bombardier who flew
thirty-five missions in a B-24 Liberator over Italy, his face
sucked tight against the gasket of the range finder,
exhausted to a zero. He ended up bombing Switzerland instead.
In the photo I have of him standing beside his crashed plane,
there's a crinkled drawing of Bugs Bunny on the fuselage,
asking, "What's up doc?"

Meanwhile David goes on telling me how God willed him
to Atlanta where he miraculously started his own business.
I closed my eyes and caught a sparkle off of Cinderella's
slipper, haloed in moonlight there on the dark stone steps,
then gave the book back to David who easily circled the words
and explained with as much weight as words could carry
how marriage needed to fly in one direction, how he needed
a woman with ambition. Said he wasn't ready yet. I remembered
washing my face a few weeks back and looking in the mirror
and seeing my face all distorted, pulled apart in five directions.
I thought finally I had glimpsed what I felt, that I saw
what I was feeling, until I realized that I was looking
into an empty paper towel dispenser that someone with good
reason, like me after my divorce, had smashed with his fist.

Now I was flying home to my new wife and kids, trying hard
to remember what I was like before I left. I wanted badly
to be what I was, if only for the family, if only for the sake
of making things smoother. David got up and was a lot shorter
than I had figured. He must've had very short legs because
through the whole trip we seemed eye-to-eye. Then he shook
my hand and quietly said his name and left. I wanted to say
that I'd write or call but I realized, really, we had nothing
at all in common and, as the surface of things took over,
people grabbing for their baggage, he melted into the line
of strangers who seemed so willing to live their lives like that.

Emerging from the walkway I caught my little son just as he
leapt flying into my arms and squealed and fervently
pressed his head against mine. Whoever I was I was home,
and I bent to kiss my wife on the lips and caught the whole
welcoming tribe of in-laws reverently lowering their heads,
and I carried my son against me for as long as I could like that.

— • • • —

Looking at Death through Bad Eyes

All of a sudden his eyes went bad
and he had to wear an ugly old pair
of old-fogey bifocals.
So he bought the glasses and began training himself:
which lens to look through at which time,
how to balance the glasses on top of his head to look busy,
how to stick them on the end of his nose to appear intense,
how to expertly flip them open when a decision had to be reached,
how to click them shut when a decision had been made,
how to hold them like a teacup when he wanted to appear pleasant,
how to suck seductively on them when he had nothing at all in mind,
how to hold them up and examine the skies for a spot,
how to clean the smudges that got all over them from his face,
and how to appear ruthless or kind or wonderful and wise
or dreamy or nervous or pompous and brutish; in short, that year,
in the middle of making himself an expert at wearing glasses,
he died.

—•—•—•—

Please, Not All at Once

I've left markers
in places where
I've left off
reading every book
in the house,
places where
my own stray thoughts
must've overpowered me,
or what I was reading,
or wished I had said,
or maybe someone
finally got through
to me. Wouldn't it be nice
if I got up now
and checked out
all those places
where I stopped
just to see if
they were all the same
word, or ended in the
beginning of some belief
or grief, or worse,
they were all different
and it all meant nothing
like letting the cat out
just as a car bomb
goes off in Beruit
on my unplugged TV?

After forty-five years of
investigations broken
off and loaded questions,
I still don't know
if I'm complex or just
above being stupid
or if at different times
I'm both. And I don't want
an answer to this but
I ask you is it or is it not
more than enough
just to know when to stop?

—•••—

From the Luxury Condo on the Sea

For three days there's been a ship
anchored in the harbor
like a word said
quietly and truly in the dark,
a word you can't take back
from the vast embattled silence
sealed by gray sky and water.

A small plume of smoke
smudges off the stern
against the steel-colored dawn
giving it the feel of a muted
Japanese scroll.
Or maybe it's on fire.

I fit my face to the binoculars,
eyes strafing, godlike,
speeding out closer, fine-tuning
the water that shivers like a mirror
chilled by flying through time.

Heavy industry, floating.
I don't know how to read the dark
mechanisms of stacks and catwalks
which, oddly, resemble a shipyard at sea,
or a prehistoric crustacean on its back,
except to imagine its insides are filled
with oil—trees and animals 100,000 years old.

Dwarfed by comparison,
off to the right,
is a small wooden lobster boat
sliding slowly in a half-circle,
like the pleasure of music,
smoothing out the water
it was made to endure.

There's a man leaning over the gunnels
hauling up dripping cages,
shredding the side of the boat
into ribbons of light
as I did once,
pulling up the writhing treasure
of mechanical black lobsters
and sometimes a shark,

like the realization of being
far out at sea
suddenly brought on board.

Out there beyond the twelve-mile limit
Russian trawlers are dragging lobsters
into steel cages the size of this room.
That's why I couldn't feed my family
and mostly took the kids for rides.

I thought there must be a way
to study the life of *Homarus americanus*
who seemed to crawl aimlessly
across the ocean floor
under the tonnage of darkness.
It must seek purpose through order
as we do and if I could determine this
I'd be a success.

I think I gave the boat away
for the memory of floating
on those glassy August mornings,
which wasn't the first time I left
something just when something else had to be done
and I ended up doing something else.

But I love this world and the way one thing
becomes another, how the impossible is pitted
against the hoping against the odds,
the freighter smoking, warming up, the man
bent over half disappearing into the sea,

the one high up putting the binoculars down
and stretching with a whole long day of nothing to do
before him, who even with the power of recall
and binoculars can't understand the difference

between here and there, now and then,
and the lobsters in their gorgeous black armor
tippling across the darkness, their eyes swiveling,
standing out on stalks, the world bearing down
and slowly moving by them with their delicate,
finely ringed antennae waving.

— • • • —

100%

I'm great, 100%, when I'm left alone
and I don't have anything to do
or have to be anything for anyone,
and no one is measuring just how little
or maladjusted I've become.

But the minute I meet humans
things get tragic.
I must have the gift to connect
right into their main switchbox
because as soon as we start kibitzing
the masks light up, the lies flicker
and ding and go bong, and the score
reaches into the billions.

It reminds me of those times
I barely lived through
when someone woke up and decided
to make a god out of Pee-Wee Herman,
and there were just a few of us left
who stayed put in our rooms during this
and then later just as I get over this
there's a conspiracy to bring back the 1950s.

So whoever it is I'm talking to
I'm just passing time, the age,
but inside I'm burning to the ground
with this anguished expression of horror
slowly developing like a Polaroid
on my face, and we're both sort of
watching this until I break it off
by screaming "Taxi!" and I get in
and the cabby throws the meter
and I can hear him telling himself
over the radio just how he's gonna
screw me. . . . Am I at some stage in my life
that nobody talks about,
something akin to how it's said
that wild animals can smell
a woman's period a mile off?

The only times the wires aren't crossed
are like when I took my cat to the vet
and asked the receptionist with latex gloves
in the glassed-in booth
with the mouth-size hole in it
how much it was gonna cost
for my cat's eighth batch of kittens
and she said, "For crissakes, fella,
whydonchagetitfixed!?"

————•—•—•————

Nothing Else

I must've been fifteen at the time
because as I'm remembering this
the same egregious feeling is beginning
to crawl through my fingertips
just itching to get back at the wheel.
And there I am all dressed up,
crammed into the backseat with the dark
and lovely Rita who, rumor had it,
would give you a feel if and when
she felt like it. And I made sure
in my sly, shy way with a particularly
suggestive orchid I pinned to her
that she did.

I don't know who was in the backseat with us
or who was driving, but there we were on our way back
from dancing the Apple Jack
to Bill Haley and the Comets, live,
and I remember the luxurious feel of her silk blouse
falling open in the dark.
I softly pushed her bra aside
and just sort of weighed them for a while.
Then I sculpted and smoothed, rounded and brooded
over them so that forever after my mind's circuitry
could flash the afterimage of them.
Rita just sort of closed her eyes and smiled.
She seemed all feeling. But she must've been thinking
of someone else since that's the last time I ever saw her.

She knew there'd be other girls who'd bring me along,
that next year I'd do 120 in my dad's convertible,
two tons of steel hurtling down an empty route,
barely touching the ground, the top ballooning
like a shout, its ecstatic grillwork lit up and grinning
like my adolescent face. That was the first and last time
I closed my eyes and thought that nothing but myself could catch me,
my licensed hands frozen to the wheel so hard I couldn't feel them.

—•—•—•—

The Radiation of Darkness

It's a sunny day
and I'm getting a tan
so I'll look good
for that someone special
I'll never meet.

But a strong wind's blowing
and I'm wondering if
the wind can blow
the rays away
so I won't get a tan.

But there must be more
to take their place
or else it'd be continual night,
chronic angst, constant dark.

I mean if the solar wind
can bend the starlight and the heart
can throw a shadow
shorter than the one
I broke my nose with
when I was learning how
to shadowbox,
doesn't that support my theory?

Because even if I'm tan
somehow I'll still be wrong
for all the women
in the world I dream of,
and that doesn't count
my Evangeline theory,
which is always occurring
whenever I turn my back.

But I think some things,
like sun and wind,
should be able to worry
about themselves,
and that, after all is said
and done, I'm natural too.
And that's something else
about which I'll have to relax.

—•••—

The BamButti: Pygmies of the Congo

This morning my woman is pulling every leaf from our hut
and is threatening to walk off to her mother's. If I stop her
in time with an apology, she will peek at me and smile and say
she has decided to take our hut down, leaf by leaf, to wash it
in the river. To us, an act performed correctly can keep death away.

We know that women own the fires of birth and death, and that men
own the shadows of things seen in daylight. That is why we start in
with our big noise about what it is to be a man and drink too many cups of
wine and boast of how we have slept with all the sweet banana girls.
There has always been much rain and much looking at rain from our huts.

For a man to be a man he must get up early one day, kick down his house,
rub ashes into the fresh cuts on his forehead, and decide to kill something
big. But for a woman, one day her breasts sprout, the moon comes down
to sleep with her, and soon she has the flow of blood and can make life.
She circles her face and breasts and buttocks with fruit paste,
puts on her powerful leaf skirt, and with the old singing and dancing
starts to hunt her man.

We men feel the way a sleeper feels when a dream is running through him.
Sometimes one of us gets brave and takes three wives into a tree.
But this is like the children's game of the snapping tree.
Everyone laughs and piles on but when the tree snaps back
he is alone in the sky and there is an end to happiness.

When the honey season ends, we blow the long molino horn which is
longer than five men and makes the sound of smoke falling through us.
It tells us that we cannot see our lives which are like our
deepest dreams which change into spirits who can outrun us.

We send the echo of the horn onto the top of the world because
our echoes are the dream of what we say, like smoke and rain,
and because whoever owns the world and whoever made us must
    want to know
that the BamButti are happy and that we are still well made.

———•••———

For most of the facts poeticized here, and for some phrasing, I am indebted to
Colin M. Turnbull's beautiful work, *The Forest People: A Study of the Pygmies
of the Congo* (Simon and Schuster, New York, 1961).

Acknowledgments

The author gratefully acknowledges the following books from which various poems in this volume appeared:

The Family War, L'Epervier Press, Fort Collins, Colorado, 1977.
© 1977 by Jack Myers
I'm Amazed That You're Still Singing, L'Epervier Press, Seattle, 1981.
© 1981 by Jack Myers
As Long as You're Happy, Graywolf Press, Saint Paul, 1986.
© 1986 by Jack Myers
Blindsided, David R. Godine, Boston, 1993.
© 1993 by Jack Myers

Some of the poems in this book also appeared in the chapbook *Coming to the Surface*, The Trilobite Press, Denton, TX, 1984. © 1984 by Jack Myers.

"Wing to Root" was first published in *Poetry*, © 1973 by The Modern Poetry Association; "Visitation Rites" was first published in *Poetry*, June 1988, © by The Modern Poetry Association.

From the section of New Poems, "The Tao of Light," "Pets," "Life Boat," and "Parable of the Burden" appeared in *The American Poetry Review*; "Now" appeared in *Poetry*, April 2000, © The Modern Poetry Association.

"The Glowing River" (frontispiece poem), appeared in *OneOnOne*, Autumn House Press, 1999.

"The BamButti: Pygmies of the Congo," was first published in *The Kenyon Review*, Spring 1990, © The Kenyon Review; "How?" was first published in *The Kenyon Review*, Summer 1990, © The Kenyon Review.

Thanks to Mark Cox and Thea Temple for their generosity, enthusiasm, and discrimination in helping me to select poems from previous books for the present work.